DON'T MESS WITH THE GODDESS

THE NEW RULES OF CONSCIOUSNESS FOR THE MILLENNIAL WOMAN

Tracey Jewel

Animal Dreaming Publishing
www.AnimalDreamingPublishing.com

Don't Mess with the Goddess

ANIMAL DREAMING PUBLISHING
PO Box 5203 East Lismore NSW 2480
AUSTRALIA
Phone +61 2 6622 6147
www.AnimalDreamingPublishing.com
www.facebook.com/AnimalDreamingPublishing

First published in 2016

Graphic Design – Rafael Baldasso
raf@pontodot.com.au

ISBN 978-0-9945248-2-9

Disclaimer
All information in this book is offered for educational purposes only. Please consider and consult professionals in the relevant field to make an educated decision as to whether suggestions in this book are right for you.

For my Daughter Grace

OVERVIEW

Don't Mess With The Goddess is the empowering guide to forging success, establishing independence and finding balance for a truly satisfying life through modern day spirituality.

This book is a lifestyle guide for all millennial women, taking a fresh holistic approach in applying certain thinking patterns and behaviours that will drastically enhance the quality of your life.

Don't Mess With The Goddess is the long awaited follow-up book from *Goddess Within* author, Tracey Jewel, who shines a light on the empowering path from goddess to domestic violence victim, to party girl and back again, and the inspirational soul lessons she learnt along the way.

Tracey Jewel shares her personal journey of how she transformed her life, offering her stories as a guidebook for discovering, embracing and inspiring a life you love to live.

Don't Mess With The Goddess shows you:

• How to make karma your bitch
• Why what you do is who you are
• What to do when you doubt everything
• How to get on the fast track to what you want
• Your Gee Spot
• CYP moments are coming

This book is a series of reflections from Tracey Jewel's very successful weekly blog with over 45,000 followers, her webinars and speaking engagements.

Contents

Overview 5

Introduction 8

A Word about Domestic Violence 10

Don't mess with the Goddess: my personal journey 12

Let the soul training begin 17

SECTION 1: GET OUT OF YOUR OWN WAY **23**

Dealing with the 'in-between' 24

Are we there yet? 25

Do you know what you want anymore? 27

Find your angry place 29

Life is what our thoughts and energy make it 31

Surrender to change 34

Stepping over setbacks 36

Turn negative energy into positive vibes 40

You're looking for obstacles instead of looking for magic 42

Karma is your bitch 44

Old ways won't open new doors 46

What is ruling you? 48

SECTION 2: THE UNIVERSE HAS YOUR BACK **51**

Babe, you got this 52

Let go of what you can't change 55

Attitude of gratitude always attracts great things 57

What is meant to be will always find a way 59

Shake it off, up or on 61

Leave a space when your _____ should go 64

Play the possibility card   67
Pick up the phone and answer the call   70
The exercise that turns _____ into reality   72
How to get back on track. Pronto. Part 1.   74
How to get back on track. Pronto. Part 2.   78

SECTION 3: YOUR POWER IS SEXY AS   **81**
Audition time is over, the curtains are open   82
What kind of bored are you?   84
The question that always brings you back to you   86
CYP moments are coming   89
The rewards of showing up   91
The element of surprise   94

SECTION 4: FIND YOUR TRIBE   97
Getting light with heavy expectations   98
How to get over FOMO (fear of missing out)   101
Find your Gee spot   104
Fill in the blanks to who you're becoming   107
Feed yourself inspiration everyday   109
Be around people who make you do better not feel better   111
There are no accidents. We meet people for a reason.   113

SECTION 5: DON'T MESS WITH THE GODDESS MANIFESTO   **115**
A Final Note   117
About the Author Tracey Jewel   119
Acknowledgements   123
Special thanks to   125

INTRODUCTION

There's something about the written word that has a way of speaking straight to your soul.

When was the last time you read something that had you lying awake at night or thinking for days? When did you last hear a saying or read a quote that gave you butterflies or that OMG yes! feeling? Seeing or hearing those words, the ones that you've been yearning for, the ones you needed to hear right in that moment, even though you didn't know it until it was right there is always inspiring, motivating—often life changing.

But what about those times when you couldn't express yourself, where you wish you knew the answers, had the words on the tip of your tongue or didn't quite know how to say the "right" thing?

For as long as I can remember, I've mused questions, scribbled down motivational quotes, saved hundreds of word tidbits in scrapbooks and surrounded myself with post-it notes as reminders. Words have always been there to refer back to whenever I needed a pick-me-up. Words pack a powerful punch, they carry vibration, energy and intention. They have a way of resonating, connecting, understanding, soothing, comforting, uplifting, encouraging and empowering.

I love the joy of words and repetition in songs, books and quotes. Words that we want to re-read, re-watch or re-listen to speak to us time and time again and never lose their value.

Don't Mess With The Goddess, at its core, isn't about stamping on your head 'Don't f*%k with me.' It's about communication and communicating who you are. In truth, love, happiness, visioning, creating, overcoming challenges and more. I hope this book speaks straight to your soul and gives you that spark you might need today.

A WORD ABOUT DOMESTIC VIOLENCE

**I was scared. I was bruised. I was isolated.
I am healing. I am hopeful.
I am one of many courageous survivors.**

One of the questions every survivor of domestic violence is posed, often incredulously, is: *Why didn't you leave?* The reality is that leaving an abusive relationship is often a herculean task that endangers the woman and calls for resources that aren't readily available.

While there are hundreds of reasons, ranging from the logistical to the deeply personal, some common themes emerge: Fear. Love. Family. Money. Shame. Isolation.

By sharing some of my story I want to stop the hurt, pain and loneliness that comes from domestic violence, because one in three women will be a victim of violence during her lifetime.

Abuse never goes away. An abuser will never change, even though he may lie dormant like a volcano for a while, let me tell you, a situation, a word, an action will erupt him again. It's only a matter of time.

We must break the cycle of abuse. It's important that women pay attention to early warning signs and that they do not stay in an abusive relationship. Women must get out and get safe.

I have a huge heart for women. I am making it my personal mission to support and speak to women every day and tell them they are worthy and beautiful.

I tell women that they have a voice. I tell women to don't let anything or anyone hold you back because your life can change others.

My life has completely transformed. When you come out on the other side after going through very difficult times, nothing seems so bad. You will see a brighter rainbow than many people do.

My life has become a beautiful transformation from ashes and tears to grace.

One woman dies every week from domestic violence in Australia, and I plan to use my voice to put an end to the silence.

DON'T MESS WITH THE GODDESS:
MY PERSONAL JOURNEY

I found myself in my usual Saturday night situation. 2am. Nightclub. Twenty people. Gathered round a table drinking from the bottle. Think Calvin Harris style. The next day I always felt hung over, half-worried, half-wobbling, half-wondering:

"How did I get here? What am I doing? Am I a fraud, or a joke? Is this really me?

Is this helpful to me or anyone else at all?"

Photos in the social circle pages of the paper. It was like tinder swiping right to the extreme of self validation of being the 'it' girl. One article in the dress circle gossip column even stated "all eyes were on Tracey Jewel".

But behind the smiles, the endless drinks and rounds of male attention, behind closed doors I would hold my hands together. Squeeze my plans. Close my eyes. Breathing deep. And breath by breath from the bottom of my lungs I found myself calling out

"I am not confused!"

And just like that ... for a few blissful, beautifully focused and productive hours ... I'm not.

Not confused. Don't mess with me. Back on track. Lock 'n' load.

"I am not confused" became my battle-cry that year. There's something arresting and magical about those four words — especially when you say them out loud, in front of people you respect.

"I am not confused" and "Don't mess with me" have become a personal mantra. Then a poem. Then a song. Then a playful writing game.

I want to share it with you. Because it's simple. Because it works. And the sooner you remember, the sooner you can get back to *your* work.

This book is all about getting back to you. What you should be doing. Who you are. For yourself and for the world.

It took getting completely off track to find I've never been more on track in my life.

Mine:

My name is Tracey Jewel. I'm a writer, speaker, writing teacher, marketeer, fempreneur, occasional poet and prolific muser.

I'm also a nester, a devoted mother and partner and "there for you always" type of friend.

Ultimately, all of my work is about helping people un-complicate the way they communicate, and do so authentically, to find their feminine voice and write with simplicity and ease. Because being understood is a beautiful thing. And if you're in business, like me, it's also a profitable thing.

That is what I do. This is who I am.

And I am not confused.

Yours:

My name is _____.

I'm a _____, _____ and.

Ultimately, all of my work is about helping people ... {choose one}

be less _____

be more _____

be amazing at _____

be more confident at _____

experience _____

feel _____

have less _____

have more _____

learn how to _____

(un)learn how to _____

reframe _____

simplify _____

start doing _____

stop doing _____

take action towards _____

understand _____

(Because _____.)

That is what I do.

And I am not confused.

**LIFE IS ALL ABOUT SOUL SEARCHING.
LOOK FOR IT WITHIN AND SHINE IT OUTWARDLY.**

LET THE SOUL TRAINING BEGIN

RULE:
THERE IS NO WAY YOU CAN CREATE A LIFE YOU LOVE WITH
AN INCONGRUENT, CLUTTERED OR NEGATIVE MIND.

WHY ARE YOU NOT DOING _____?

RULE:

MAKE IT UN-IGNORABLE, UNSTOPPABLE AND FIGURE-OUTABLE

When it comes to doing that one thing you want to do, the huge soul search can be daunting if not a little overrated. At some point (and the earlier the better) you should just start doing something. Anything!

For me, well I wanted to write and I wasn't. Instead I was in the vicinity of writing. I worked in others' bookstores, I started my own bookstore, hell I even joined writers' groups and book clubs, everything but writing for myself.

I wrote down on my to do list 'write'. It's right there, I saw it every time I walked in my house. Yet... I wasn't doing it.

Not just for writing, or for the career you should be pursuing, this is for all types of goals. It's a painful cycle to be in and it happens to everyone at some point.

The problem with trying to figure out what you should be doing is that it takes forever. Knowing what to do is not an end game, it can be infinite. Trying to 'know oneself' before 'doing' guarantees no right answer.

So I have two questions you can ask yourself:

1. Do you actually want to _____

<insert what you want to do here>?

It's perfectly okay if the answer is actually no, I don't know, maybe or hell yeah!

And you know why? Because there are hundreds of thousands of other things you can do instead! If it's anything but a hell yeah, bench it and move onto the next thing you want to do.

2. Are you willing to be crazy immersed, ridiculously enthused and take massive action about the thing you want to do?

When I say crazy and ridiculous I mean are you willing to take risks, disrupt your life, create space and new habits to include it in your world?

When I was studying English Lit in school, I became obsessed with the subject to the point of letting my other subjects slide.

I wanted to be able to recite word for word Henrick Ibsen's *A Doll's House*, I was obsessed with *The Remains of the Day* and dreamt about *How to kill a mockingbird*. I was cray cray. I literally had post-it notes of phrases and quotes on every square inch of my room. It was in my blood. And as much as I studied, learnt and absorbed it was never enough. But I needed to do it to accomplish my goal of being the best in my school.

That's what I mean about doing something. What are you actually willing to do?

And by the way, it worked – I won the state prize in English Lit (thank god, as I pretty much barely passed the other subjects and they let me into university anyway!)

Writing down what you want to do or talking about it with a friend is just not going to cut it.

If you want it bad enough you're going to have to do more than talk and write about it.

Make doing part of your energy, your environment; make it so epic that you can't not do it.

You want to write? Buy some journals and pens and put them in every room.

Want to get fit? Sleep in your gym gear so you're ready to go when you wake up.

Want a new career? Write out your new CV and job list on a massive sheet of paper and hang it from the end of your bed.

Get my point?

My friend Cara says, "If you want to provoke change and make big things happen, passion isn't enough. You've got to be unreasonable."

Another friend Em says, "Your life is worth making a scene over."

Make that thing you want to do unstoppable, un-ignorable and in your face. Literally.

It's going to be so worth it. Get to know the feeling of doing exactly what you say you're going to do and own it with every ounce of your being.

GET OUT OF YOUR OWN WAY

DEALING WITH THE 'IN-BETWEEN'

RULE:

BE IN BETWEEN WHO YOU ARE AND WHO YOU WANT TO BE, NOT WHO YOU THINK YOU SHOULD BE.

Are we there yet?

If you have goals and plans for your life and your future, you've probably been at the 'in-between' stage more than a few times, not yet seeing the fruits of your labour.

It's all well and good to be ambitious and excited at the goal-setting stage but usually when you're in the throes of it or waiting on the sidelines for the next step you're what I call the in-between. You are feeling frustrated and stuck, like you're not making progress fast enough.

In the in-between we worry. We go over our plan again. And again. We feel like a mouse on a wheel.

The good news is to get to the in-between, you've probably passed a major milestone.

But eventually, at some point life will move you on from this stage too.

But 'eventually' and 'some point' are scary words. What does it mean? Sooner rather than later? One month? One year? Longer?

Not knowing the exact timeframe can make you crazy asking, what now?

But what about enjoying it? Enjoying the uncertainty. Revel in it. Bathe in it. Be happy about it!

You will never be in exactly this same in-between stage ever again in your life (although, you will be in others, for sure).

Enjoying really just means accepting. Accept the uncertainty, knowing that you've done the planning, you're doing the work, and eventually (that scary word) things will come together for you.

How do you possibly enjoy the in-between?

First off, *know* that it's the in-between. Know that you won't be here forever. Know that this is a temporary state. Imagine how things will be in your new state, knowing that will come.

Secondly, do things that make you happy during this stage. What makes you happy and appreciate life? What makes you feel nurtured and taken care of? What makes you lose track of time and feel carefree?

Make a list if you have to. Now do those things! If you love to run, take time out every day or every other day for that. If phoning a long-time friend makes you feel good, do that daily. Like weekly manicures and monthly massages? If you can make that happen, sure...whatever it takes!

And most importantly, keep the faith.

At this point, more than ever, you need to believe that you have the power to take yourself to the next step. Know that it's just a matter of time.

So accept the present uncertainty. Who knows what will come after this?

Oh right, *you* do: your end goal, the thing you've been working toward, with patience throughout the process. If you embrace this in-between phase, the reward will be even sweeter.

DO YOU KNOW WHAT YOU WANT ANYMORE?

RULE:
IT USUALLY ISN'T NOT KNOWING WHAT YOU WANT.
IT'S THINKING THAT YOU *SHOULD* KNOW WHAT YOU WANT.

When you think you should know, you put the pressure on.

When you accept things for today as it is, it frees up your energy.

When you question what you want it's usually because your desires and vision are clouded by fears.

The solution lies in seeing through these fears for what they really are. False.

What would happen if you stepped forward regardless of your fear?

From action, you will sense what's right and what you want.

What we really want can never be put out. They can be dampened and dismissed, but never extinguished.

This isn't about picking the right thing. It's picking right now.

And right now, it's about simply learning to follow your interests, regardless of fear.

FIND YOUR ANGRY PLACE

RULE:

IF SOMEONE CAN EASILY ANGER YOU,
YOU'RE OFF BALANCE WITHIN YOURSELF.

How many times do we get told to ""go to your happy place" when we are in stressful situations?

When I'm in a tense boardroom meeting, a confronting conversation or trying to do 20 kettlebell squats, the last thing that's going to help me is going to my 'happy place'. I want to get angry.

Do you even have an angry place?

I started thinking about my friend, who was amazing at her job, getting made redundant at the drop of a hat. Angry place

I thought about my mum staring down the barrel of a quadruple heart bypass. Very angry place.

Next time I was in a stressful situation I thought about these and said, "This one's for you," and I got through that situation like my life depended on it.

Turns out my angry place is a great place to be. Rather than faking it through trying to be happy, feel your anger rather than supress it.

Channel your anger, let it burn and direct it to getting through a tough spot. It's like gas for your goals.

LIFE IS WHAT OUR THOUGHTS AND ENERGY MAKE IT

RULE:
CHANGE YOUR THOUGHTS. CHANGE YOUR WORLD.

She sees business possibilities everywhere. You see business as confinement that makes it difficult for you to flourish.

They see nice people who want to help out. You see selfish people, only looking out for themselves.

He saw a glamorous plane trip to Paris. You saw carbon emissions, wrecking our planet.

And so on.

We all have these thoughts. There are times my loved ones have these thoughts and I want to shake them and say, "Brighten up! Life is meant to be enjoyed!"

And I'm sure there are days where my friends want to shake me and say, "Open your eyes! Not everyone has what you have!"

It's not about right or wrong. It's about a peaceful equilibrium with your thoughts.

A place in the middle where your thoughts and your energy can co-exist.

Vent your frustration about the flat tyre. The broken drawer. The Global Financial Crisis or poverty. Then create balance, name things you are grateful for.

Set some new rules around your thoughts and the energy you want to permeate.

Rules like:

No matter what happened today, I will end this day on a positive note. I will not check Facebook until midday. Sunday is no work day for doing fun things – no seriousness allowed.

Your thoughts and your energy can work together like the dark and the light work together. Opposite powers, yet both equally necessary.

Working, together, for a better world.

SURRENDER TO CHANGE

RULE:
CHANGE THE CHANNEL

Sometime it feels exhausting and pretty much impossible to change our thoughts. The thing is we have to start thinking differently before we can do something different.

So how about changing the channel instead?

A channel, just like on your TV, is a way of receiving information that informs us what we watch or, in life's case, how we think and behave. Moving is a channel. Dreaming is a channel. Language and words are channels. It's like a Netflix of choices streaming through us!

When we purposefully start choosing the channel we want, we interrupt our pattern, our habits. I mean, what happens when we don't like what's on TV? We change the channel!

By being in control of the remote so to speak, you'll soon find that you start thinking, "Why am I telling myself that I have to do this? Clearly, I'm choosing to."

Being a journey rather than *Being ON a journey.*

Because I want people to think differently about starting something new. To *be on a journey* conjures up the end result. To be 'on' something means there's 'on' and then there's 'off'. With that, there's a lot of to-dos and pressure.

However, to *be something* can be continuous: we're always being something, whether or not we're choosing what to be with consciousness.

STEPPING OVER SETBACKS

RULE:

SETBACKS SHOW YOU HOW CLOSE YOU ARE
TO ACHIEVING YOUR DREAMS.

Just when you think you are ready to get some ideas into motion and action, you have a setback.

Setbacks can involve finances (unexpected bills, for example), time delays, or even an unresponsive partner or friend when you want to make changes. Sometimes it's a health scare.

At that moment of action, when all your hard work starts to pay off, a little voice creeps in to stop you from moving forward. It creates doubt and makes you question your decisions.

Facing and dealing with setbacks is a part of life for all of us. And sometimes when we think we're ready to unleash on the world, the universe has other plans!

We can choose, however, to find something good in our setbacks. It all depends on what we want to take from them.

If you're dealing with a setback:

1. Acknowledge it.

No one is immune to setbacks. If you have one, recognise the problem. By doing this you can start the process of transformation, for it is on the other side of the setback that we realise we are not going to be the same person we were before. We are going to be wiser, stronger, and better for it.

Like nature and the seasons, the caterpillar and the butterfly, the tadpole and the frog, there's no turning back, there's no putting our head in the sand to pretend it isn't happening. Acknowledge that through the tough times, the miracles of transformation happen, and we can flourish on the other side.

We are capable of doing amazing things—and even more if we can grow through our challenges.

2. Eliminate blame.

Things happen for no obvious reason sometimes. Exploring the way forward is much healthier than trying to blame someone or something for a setback that is irreversible.

3. Access your spirituality.

Spirituality can sustain us in times of uncertainty and difficulty. When we feel like we don't have the physical, mental, or emotional strength to pull through, our faith in something more—whatever that may be—gives us the energy we need to keep going.

Spirituality reminds us that we are a gift, and have gifts to offer the world. Our job right now is to discover these gifts and to remove the setbacks so we can give them to others in the future.

Focusing on our spirituality allows us to see beyond this setback and find a purpose for it.

4. Give yourself time.

Just as we need to allow time for wounds and broken hearts to mend, we need to allow ourselves time to overcome our setbacks. Impatience only makes them harder and longer than they need to be.

We are in such a hurry to fix our problems and move on, and usually this impatience is a pattern that overflows into other areas of our life.

I am terribly guilty of impatience, and the only solution I have found is focusing on and enjoying other things while allowing a setback to be resolved in its own time. I try to remember what really matters. I think back to happy memories and keep faith that after this setback I will be where I want to be.

It serves no purpose to dwell on a problem. Allow the movement of time to push you through it. Time does heal!

5. Step out of your comfort zone.

This is what I am doing now—confronting and staring a setback in the face, and sharing it honestly to say, "Hey this is where I'm at." This type of openness has enormous power. We can learn so much from other people who are dealing with their own challenges, but we have to share our own to do it.

I'm dealing with a health challenge now, but I am not a victim. Setbacks can be overcome—even sickness.

I know I will be in a better situation on the other side of this, especially if I hold onto my faith and joy. I am confident I can beat this!

Yes we are all going to deal with setbacks in life, but we can overcome them if we see them as part of a bigger life picture, and commit to seeing them through from start to finish. Remember that this setback won't stop you from being who you want to be or doing what you want to do.

TURN NEGATIVE ENERGY INTO POSITIVE VIBES

RULE:

POSITIVE PEOPLE ARE DRAWN TO *POSITIVE ENERGY*;
NEGATIVE PEOPLE ARE DRAWN TO NEGATIVE ENERGY.

Do you complain? Do you discuss what's wrong rather than what's right? Are you attracted to drama? Do you feel like you're not in control? Do you feel like things are happening to you? Or through you?

Your answers may show you where your negativity radar is. And a radar can be adjusted.

Negativity not only affects us but everyone around us. Negativity has a tangible effect on our health, resulting in more stress and sickness than those who choose to live positively.

When we make the decision to be positive, we begin to encounter situations and people that are also positive. The negative energy gets edged out by all the positive experiences. Although negative and positive thoughts will always exist, the key to becoming positive is to limit the amount of negativity that we experience by filling ourselves up with more positivity.

Have you noticed that positive people seem to get what they want out of life? Even if things don't go their way, *they still enjoy their lives.*

Replacing or removing negative thoughts with positive ones does take practice. It's about catching yourself out and changing your tune.

Become more positive and you will find you have more control over your circumstances than you believe and soon you will begin to consciously design a positive life.

YOU'RE LOOKING FOR OBSTACLES INSTEAD OF LOOKING FOR MAGIC

RULE:

STOP GIVING YOUR OBSTACLES PERMISSION
TO BLOCK YOUR DREAMS.

Obstacles only have power if you give them power.

If obstacles become an 'if they happen' not a 'when they happen' you stop searching for them.

And 'if' they do?

Position your progress as Marie Forleo always says is figuroutable. You'll find a way. You'll see it as just something to push through, like going on a bear hunt.

Remain unwilling to see anything as an obstacle, then you'll be looking for solutions, not excuses.

Of course you can do it.

The question is, will you?

KARMA IS YOUR BITCH

RULE:
TAKE FULL RESPONSIBILITY; STOP BEING THE VICTIM.

You are responsible for your thoughts. People who consistently believe that things happen *to* them handicap themselves to a victim mentality. This is a subtle and deceptive negative thought pattern. Phrases like "I *have* to work" or "I can't believe he did that *to* me" are indicators of a victim mentality. Blaming circumstances and blaming others only handicaps our decision to change something negative into something positive.

Taking full responsibility for your life, your thoughts and your actions is one of the biggest steps in creating a more positive life. We have unlimited potential within to create our own reality, change our life, and change our thoughts. When we begin to really internalise this we discover that no one can make us feel or do anything. We choose our emotional and behavioural response to people and circumstances.

Make positive choices in favour of yourself.

OLD WAYS WON'T
OPEN NEW DOORS

RULE:
CLOSE SOME DOORS.

Heard that the definition of insanity is doing the same thing over and over and expecting a different result?

Old ways could involve hesitation, procrastination, self doubt and other behaviours you want to close the door on for good.

New ways could involve embracing change, self worth, remembering choices and saying yes.

Paint a picture of old and new and what words you would use. Close the door on the old and open the new.

But remember new doors won't open by themselves.

WHAT IS RULING YOU?

RULE:
RULE YOUR ENERGY OR OTHERS WILL RULE IT FOR YOU.

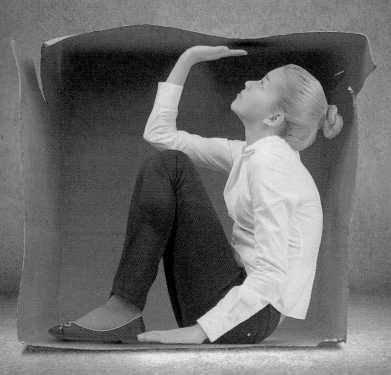

Most of us are encouraged to control, put our confidence in or look outside of ourselves—our parents, our husband, our boss. Maybe it's a political party or a group of friends.

We're taught to believe that if we play by the rules we will win. If you go to a good university or school you'll get a good job. If you follow a particular church or religion your life will be worth more. If you climb the ladder in your corporate job, you will have career advancement and be able to retire with money.

These things that seem to rule our lives are often not the kind that bring us closer to who we want to be on a soul level.

These rules don't always bring happiness or the feelings of being alive. And sometimes these rules deprive us of energy. Because we have to compromise ourselves, our truth and what we want.

Ruling yourself and your energy first above external expectations can be a difficult journey. How are we supposed to choose ourselves with no track record?

Especially when no one else believes like you do, and you don't see anyone else making the choice to choose for themselves their own rules over the expectations of others.

Making your own rules and ruling your own energy is a requirement for any woman who truly wants to live her destiny. Our true nature can't live in a world of everyone else's rules to follow.

We must make our rules, desires and decisions our north star.

THE UNIVERSE HAS YOUR BACK

BABE, YOU GOT THIS

RULE:

TAKE A LEAP OF FAITH AND THE UNIVERSE WILL BE
THERE TO CATCH YOU.

When was the last time you took a leap of faith?

The kind that makes the universe shake with you and shows you along the way the little signs and signals that you are on the right track.

Taking this big leap may leave you with feelings of gratitude, trembling with fear or even exploding with happiness that you took it. Or all of these things at once.

Taking a big leap makes you feel alive.

And because you took the leap, your life, your future, the game changed forever.

And all the leap really is... is having faith in yourself.

We're not taught what taking a leap in life, in faith, actually is or what it even means, let alone how to do it.

Stepping outside our comfort zone, change making, thought leading, recreating our life is still deemed unconventional. But it's these big leaps that make headlines.

Think of Malala.

Think of Maya Angelou, who had been born to poverty and abuse, worked as a fry cook, a prostitute, and a nightclub dancer. She somehow found the courage to write her first book, then many more, and ended up being honoured by reading a poem at Obama's inauguration and earning 50 honorary degrees in her lifetime.

When women take little leaps or big leaps, collaboratively they quietly change their world, and we all benefit.

Taking a leap is not a given. It's not a simple task. And sometimes it doesn't even feel like an option. It requires contemplation, courage, backing oneself, speaking out, taking a risk and standing tall. And most of all it requires practice so we continue to take bigger and bigger leaps, again and again.

Be it a tiny leap or a massive game-changing leap – you have the choice to trust and reach for your desire, right now.

LET GO OF WHAT YOU CAN'T CHANGE

RULE:

FROZEN MAY BE ONTO SOMETHING SINGING "LET IT GO."

Do you find yourself repeating the same conversations, frustrations, complaints to different people? You go over and over in your mind what you should have done. Or what someone else should have done. You are future planning on what could be or how to make someone else do or force something.

Letting go involves making a change but it doesn't mean giving up.

We can make a different choice. Start with the choice to let go of all the things you can't control and start using your time to master what you can.

ATTITUDE OF GRATITUDE ALWAYS ATTRACTS GREAT THINGS

RULE:

BECOME GRATEFUL—FOR EVERYTHING.

When life is all about us, it's just about entitlement.

Living in this entitlement full time, people become an 'energy sucker'. And what energy can be attracted by sucking rather than giving? You can't live a positive life this way.

When life comes from a place of being grateful and appreciative, from the small challenges, to the car that gets us everywhere, to a major backslide to an upswing. We shift our attitude from one of selfishness to one of appreciation.

This appreciation energy shift gets noticed by others, and like a ripple effect begins to form positivity in our relationships.

We begin to receive more. We attract great things. Not just for us but for others too.

WHAT IS MEANT TO BE WILL ALWAYS FIND A WAY

RULE:

THERE ARE MOMENTS AND EVENTS IN OUR LIVES
THAT ARE MEANT TO HAPPEN IN ORDER TO GET US
WHERE WE ARE MEANT TO BE.

Sometimes the simplest of things can catch our attention and leave us with the perfect message that we so needed to hear. It's in these moments that something shifts, we have a moment of clarity or a goose bump and a tingle and we know our line of fate has changed forever.

These moments guide us in the direction we need to go.

We need to believe and trust these deep down feelings that the universe conspires not so things become a matter of if, but of when and how.

It's not that we didn't know what we want, it's more that we need a reminder or confirmation that it's going to happen. They provide reassurance of what we are looking for.

Here are some favourite quotes of reassurance:

Difficult roads often lead to beautiful destinations.

We are sometimes taken into troubled waters not to be drowned but to be cleansed.

And suddenly you just know, it's time to start something new and trust the magic of beginnings. ~ Meister Eckhart

Faith and fear both demand you believe in something you cannot see. You choose. ~ Bob Proctor

It might take a year, it might take a day but what's meant to be will always find a way.

SHAKE IT OFF,
UP OR ON

RULE:
WHEN YOU'RE UNSURE OF EVERYTHING,
EVERYTHING IS POSSIBLE.

I am addicted to Spotify and the ability to shuffle, create and follow playlists depending on my mood.

After discussing this with several friends and my love for random music taste I noticed a trend.

My 'safe' friends never shuffled, they liked to know what song was next. They carefully selected every song, listened to an album in order and the songs all the way through. Yawn.

We all have different risk profiles and the small trends of Do you shuffle your music? Do you take a different route to work every day? Do you order the same coffee every time? speak volumes and all these show a part of who you are and if you are driven by stability or variety.

Anthony Robbins quotes many times that the quality of your life is in direct proportion to the amount of uncertainty you can comfortably deal with.

Uncertainty is going to crop up anyway so wouldn't it be nice to find a way to comfortably live with more of it?

I can embrace uncertainty by _____

_____

_____

_____

_____

What is the fear of _____ trying to tell me?

I can improve my tolerance of uncertainty by _____

_____

_____

_____

I can reduce uncertainty by _____

_____

_____

_____

I will try _____

as something different

Start small. Shake up your routine. You'll be surprised how life can change with subtle varieties.

LEAVE A SPACE WHEN YOUR ___ SHOULD GO

RULE:
ALWAYS MAKE ROOM FOR SPACE IN YOUR LIFE.

I'm by no means a designer but I certainly am a minimalist. I'm not afraid of having white space in my home.

It's space that isn't filled with things and a concept I try to overflow into other areas of my life that I struggle with.

We fill in space by checking Facebook, doing things others want us to do and pretty much wasting time.

White space can be used to design our life, creating balance and prioritising. It can also be the space where possibility lies that cannot become reality in a cramped life.

I have a study in my home with an antique desk and white wooden bookcase that I love. However, it has a hideous old hand-me-down reading chair that I hate looking at, let alone sitting in.

A girlfriend of mine commented that unless I get rid of it, the perfect chair won't show up. Good point. So I did, after some resistance of "There will be a big hole in the room. What will I sit on?" and so forth.

Every time I walked in I thought about the new chair and how it was going to feel. And she was right. Within a few weeks I found the perfect reading chair with calligraphy fabric and comfy arm rests.

Letting go and allowing space makes the way for something better, something more beautiful. Always.

What are you giving up space to that isn't valuable to you?

Allow for space where your finest _____ should go.

I can create _____ space in my physical world.

I can create _____ space in my digital world.

I can create _____ space in my mental world.

I can create _____ space in my emotional world.

Clear space. Allow for possibility. Everywhere.

PLAY THE
POSSIBILITY CARD

RULE:
WEAR POSSIBILITY GLASSES. SEE IT EVERYWHERE.

It's always easier to come up with reasons not to do something. Also known as excuses.

It easy to say it's impossible and forget what is possible and even easier to remind our friends of this than ourselves. See things as possible and the walls will start tumbling down.

Write yourself a list from the eyes of a world of possibility.

I see myself _____

_____

_____

_____

_____

_____

I see you and me _____

_____

_____

_____

_____

_____

I see me finally starting/quitting/putting/making/recording/
disovering/walking/publishing (you get the drift)

_____

_____

_____

_____

_____

_____

_____

_____

See yourself astonishing you with what's possible. And just see
what comes next.

PICK UP THE PHONE AND ANSWER THE CALL

RULE:
IF YOU'RE BEING CALLED, ANSWER IT.

Whatever it is calling you...

To go off the grid. To pull the escape cord. To a holiday destination, to a city, to a tribe. To pull out of a class. To start a class. To tear down a wall. To paint a room. To dump the asshole. To ask that guy out. To flirt. To hug more. To skip the party. To gate crash the party. To cancel the wedding. To sell the ring.

To hit the snooze button. To get up 15 minutes earlier. To say goodbye. To make amends. To book the appointment. To buy that bag. Those shoes. To open that book. To flip the page.

To launch the business, to double your rates, to throw out your business cards, to say hell no. To say a hundred times yes.

Just answer the call.

THE EXERCISE THAT TURNS _____ INTO REALITY

RULE:

USE YOUR IMAGINATION.

Everything starts in the mind and imagination. It is responsible for the life you are experiencing and will create your future.

A business started as a thought and mental image. A new car started with the thought of you purchasing and possessing it. Losing weight starts with imagining being slim and toned.

When you imagine a certain thing, after a while you start thinking about it most of the time. This leads to driving you to search for information about it, becoming aware of opportunities that could make it a reality, and taking action and being motivated to accomplish what you imagined.

Soon enough your imagination affects your reality. Your thoughts start affecting the thoughts of other people and attract people who think like you and can help you.

It is not a coincidence that when you are looking desperately for an object, an answer or an expert, all of a sudden the object or the answer pops up, or you find the person you are looking for.

Through your imagination, you are shaping your life's events.

Imagination can start by simple answering the question: "Wouldn't it be great if..."

When you learn to be in control of your imagination, you control your destiny.

HOW TO GET BACK ON TRACK. PRONTO. PART 1.

RULE:

FOLLOW THE WARNING SIGNS. WHEN YOU'RE
OFF TRACK YOU'RE ACTUALLY SO CLOSE TO BEING
MORE ON TRACK THAN EVER BEFORE.

What's my purpose? What am I looking for? Where am I going with my life? What is my direction?

Big stuff.

You may be doing 'okay'. You may have a good job. A supportive family. Close friends. A home. Or you may be in the shit with your own fair share of struggles.

Either way the picture of your life doesn't feel enough. It doesn't feel 'on track'.

You vow to make New Year's resolutions. You vow to change your life. You vow to go after your dreams. Vow to quit your job, join that book club or start your own business.

Vow and vow and then one, two, five years go by. You take stock of where you are. And you still feel off track. You reach a little. You pull back. You jump tracks. You hitch another train ride. You break your vows a hundred times.

So how do you find your track? Your direction? How do you start again after breaking your vows?

There are two important parts to this.

The first is to know the warning signs and the feelings of being off track before you can change and choose a different direction. The second is to make a decision and start.

Here are five warning signs you're on the wrong track and what to do about it.

1. All the decisions you've made, someone else has made for you.

You've got to stop caring about what everyone else wants for you and live for yourself. Don't hide behind other people's decisions. Find your love, your talents, your passions and own them. The life you create from doing something that moves you is far better than the life you get from sitting around wishing you were doing.

2. You're only making the safe decisions.

Never let fear decide your future for you. Playing it too safe can actually be the riskiest track to take. Growth doesn't come from playing safe, it comes from change and being out of your comfort zone.

Yes, accept the track you're on but let go of what was and focus on what could be. Every step forward will be worth it. It's the steps that give meaning to life.

3. Your track is full of obstacles.

The only difference between an obstacle and an opportunity is how you look at it. If you keep your head down, you'll miss all the different life tracks that are out there.

Look at situations where you can make a difference, look at an environment where you can reach great heights. Pull along a positive 'reality' of what's possible along whatever track you choose and it will be the right one.

4. You work so damn hard but there's no headway.

We as humans have constraints of limited time and limited energy. It's critical to spend these resources and others effectively. Do the right work instead of doing a bunch of work and stuff. Don't confuse being productive with being busy.

Same goes for doing a bunch of different things and completing none of them. How you feel about being on the 'right track' will be decided on what we finish, not what we start.

5. People and their energy are dragging you off track.

Wrong tracks can happen when you worry and trust the wrong people. Don't make time for people who don't make time for you. With these types of people, you affected their life, don't let them affect yours. Don't get side-tracked by people who are not on track.

Be responsible for your own energy. Know your worth. Surround yourself with people that light you up, who support you no matter what track you're on.

The second part is this: your present actions can instantly steer you onto the right track. From this moment forward everything changes if you want it to. You simply have to decide what to do right now. And do it.

HOW TO GET BACK ON TRACK. PRONTO. PART 2.

RULE:

EVERYTHING CHANGES NOW IF YOU SAY SO.

Once you've figured out you've been backsliding onto the wrong track for one day, two months, three years, four or more...

Oops.

However long you've been in a slump, skipping out and feeling totally unenthused, just not into it, it's time to get back on track and back into routine.

It's hard to reboot after a lull, even it's a short one but there's an easier way to get back on track for anything that deeply matters to you.

The change starts today. Be firm and tough about that today, not tomorrow.

Schedule the change today. Make it non-negotiable and uncancellable.

Remind yourself this does matter. It's never too late.

Today is not over yet.

YOUR POWER IS SEXY AS

AUDITION TIME IS OVER, THE CURTAINS ARE OPEN

RULE:

IT'S SHOW TIME. ALWAYS.

I'm sure you've heard the saying that with life, there is no dress rehearsal. Well guess what? It isn't a rehearsal. It's not even an audition. You know why? You've already got the part. So give it your best shot.

I was a professional ballet dancer for a few years and started ballet when I was four years old. My childhood was filled with endless disciplined hours on the barre or in pointe shoes and I have the feet to prove it. I didn't quite appreciate the practice of ballet then. I do now. And I'm so grateful.

I 'retired', for want of a better word, in my early twenties and began trying different vocations, studies and jobs. I saw a new facet of my being emerge – that of a writer and mentor.

And through my ballet experience a lesson emerged: life is a performance, and the world is your stage, your platform.

We think we audition for many things – first dates, job interviews, dazzling a boss or our peers and we have a human tendency to hold back, withdraw, restrain.

This 'audition' thinking has given us the idea that life is a rehearsal so we don't really give it our best shot. Are we really going to get the part by just trying out?

What if we went into these situations not as an audition but with the mindset of a standing ovation on opening night? What if we just took the stage, wore our best dress and embodied the role, owned it? Do you see a director taking notes on your life performance?

If you carry yourself through life like you already have the part no one will see you as anything but.

And then do it again. And again. From the top. Don't hold back.

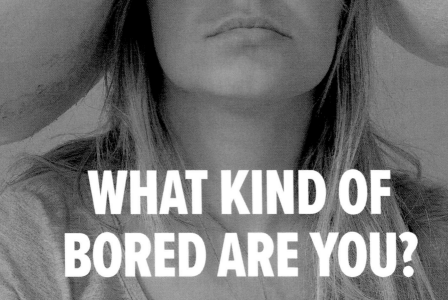

WHAT KIND OF BORED ARE YOU?

RULE:

BEING BORED IS A LACK OF BEING CREATIVE. A LACK OF BEING CRAZY. A LACK OF BEING.

Feeling blah. We've all been there.

It could be your job that doesn't inspire. Your relationship leaves you feeling numb. Your home doesn't feel like...well, home.

You want to find something to be passionate about, something that makes you feel alive. And the key lies in your boredom.

Sometimes I find myself in blahness, feeling fuzzy about who I am and what I'm doing, mislabelling moments and getting deeply distracted.

Brushing off boredom won't stop it.

Answering the question *why*? will.

What are you tired of?

What are you done to death of doing?

What are you bummed about?

Why are you burnt out?

When you admit what's boring you, you can focus on what's exciting and compelling instead.

Write a list of what's boring you and what you're not bored with. And if writing lists bores you maybe chat to a friend instead.

THE QUESTION THAT ALWAYS BRINGS YOU BACK TO YOU

RULE:

LIFE IS ALWAYS UNDER CONSTRUCTION, THERE'S ALWAYS SOMETHING TO IMPROVE.

It's a sickening feeling when something blindsides you, when you don't see 'it' coming. 'It' could be a redundancy, a break up or even something as simple as getting to the end of the day and asking yourself "What the F have I actually accomplished today?"

I have found myself in a position before where I was killing it at work, thinking my role was bulletproof when suddenly redundancies were being made left, right and centre. I had no Plan B as I was so sure my Plan A would work out.

The most terrifying part wasn't the prospect of no income or the uncertainty of my future or even the complete lack of any idea of what I was going to do next. Oh no. It was the fear of making the wrong choice, the wrong next decision. The fear of that which would lead to not becoming who I wanted to be in the world.

What did this equal? Feelings of being overwhelmed and not making a decision.

Not feelings I enjoy.

Now my dad's an architect and is always good for some direct, logical and sound advice in situations like these (it was either that or my tarot cards).

He asked me, "What are you building? What are you designing?"

Those words almost shook the wine from my hand.

I knew the answer straight away. Write, create, mentor. That's the world I want to design and build.

And what was the slap in the face? I'd been using tools, bricks and plans that weren't for my own building.There's nothing wrong with these tools, they are just not for my building, they're for someone else's. I've been building someone else's dream house.

Since that chat with my dad I've been a much better architect of my own life.

Construction is back on schedule.

CYP MOMENTS ARE COMING

Driving down a highway with the wind blowing through my hair... walking along the beach breathing in the air.... nailing a boardroom presentation... finishing a crazy hard gym session... these are CYP (cream your panties) feeling moments for me that life just doesn't get better than this.

Feelings of opportunity. Of possibility. Of exploring. Of experiencing. All CYP moments for your soul.

What is something that lights you up? What makes your heart race? What makes you feel free? What drives you? What fills you up with possibility?

CYP moments that light you up are something to fight for, pursue and bring into your life on a regular basis.

If it's been a while since you've experienced a moment like this go back to a time when you felt truly inspired and happy. Picture it in your mind, then answer:

What were you doing?
Who were you with (if with anyone)?
What were you saying to yourself?
What were you saying to the other person (if with anyone)?
Where were you?
What were you hearing?
How were you holding yourself?
What could you see?
What colours were around you?

Do this as many times as you need.

Now ask yourself, **what were the similar themes in each of these moments?** Circle the things that stand out.

And then ask, **how can I bring these experiences, feelings, drive back into my life right now?**

As soon as you know what lights you up and how, the sooner you can experience it as often as possible.

If you can fill your life with CYP moments that light you up, the happier you can be.

THE REWARDS OF SHOWING UP

RULE:

LIFE IS TOO SHORT NOT TO SHOW UP

There was a time in my life where I thought I was putting myself 'out there' but I didn't get invited to events, parties, dates or anything. The universe and people were not reciprocating. It felt like the world was passing me by.

I got so tired of waiting I just decided to show up. I didn't have to wait to be invited. I didn't even RSVP. I went from being a chronic no show to the life of the party.

There is no substitute for showing up.

It doesn't matter what you're creating — a book, a business, a potential new relationship, an entirely new way of being...

You can read every guide, take every course, watch every tutorial, hire every expert, research, vision-board, dream and scheme. But there's no replacement for showing up.

Commit to showing up.

Want to know what you're committed to? Look at your calendar. Examine how you spend your time and who with.

If you 'can't find the time' to do what you want to do. DO something else. But be honest about what you're committed to showing up for.

And on a side digital note: posting on Facebook is a version of showing up but it's not very world engaging now is it? Or if you show up to something and spend the whole time posting about wit on Facebook, isn't engaging either is it?

Lets nail down showing up for real:

I am showing up _____

I show up in my _____

by_____.

_____ keeps me from showing up.

It means _____ to me to show up.

Right now I can't show up _____.

Show up for you because this party isn't going to go on forever...

Accept this as your personal invitation.

THE ELEMENT OF SURPRISE

SURPRISE

RULE:
GO ON, DO IT, YOU MAY SURPRISE YOURSELF

If you're having trouble with an area of your life, attack it when _____ isn't expecting it.

Have you had an absolutely impossible week? Project? Partner?

The kind of _____ and you have a kind of anxiety attack?

You think to yourself there is no way you're going to get through the deadline, argument, responsibility.

You feel like it's going to wipe you out with what's coming.

Or... you might just surprise yourself. After all, you have a 100 per cent success rate of getting through every bad day so far yes?!

Some of the best nights, experiences and things in life are unplanned. The ones you don't expect. Surprises can bring opportunities, people and amazing randomness into your life you never knew was there.

Get yourself into situations where you can be surprised. Look forward to the unknown. Be open to the unusual. Search for something that will add richness to your life.

Wow what an option. And remember surprise birthdays are always fun ☺

FIND YOUR TRIBE

GETTING LIGHT WITH HEAVY EXPECTATIONS

RULE:

EXPECT NOTHING. APPRECIATE EVERYTHING

"You have amazing potential. You are going to do great things with your life." Heard these expectations before? But you feel like you're not accomplishing any great feats and not fulfilling your potential.

Being capable, gifted and talented, which we all are in some way, should be a joy and a privilege but can become toxic.

Expectations to be more and do more can make you feel inadequate. Craving more with anything less becoming a failure. Our patterns of dissatisfaction are unsustainable. We need to get light on the heavy.

And the easiest way to throw down our burden is to focus on others, not on ourselves. Seek satisfaction through your personal relationships.

You will soon find we all have these similar issues of inadequacy. You are not alone.

These people around you are beautiful and good, inadequacies and all, then you must be good too.

By loving others, you have already achieved a purpose.

At the end of the day, people simply want to receive love and attention; and through giving others these things you not only improve their lives, but you own perception and expectations of yourself.

Instead of potential, focus on the immediate positive impact your life can make on others.

The truth is, not everyone can change the world, and not everyone needs to. All we can do is give as much love in our lives as possible, treat ourselves kindly, and leave the world a more positive place than when we entered it.

That is all I can ask of myself, and I try to leave all other expectations of myself behind—the ones of impermanent success that can only bring me dissatisfaction and suffering.

Maybe thousands do not know your name, but you have the power to completely change the lives of those around you with love, and that, I've learned, is far more gratifying and important.

HOW TO GET OVER FOMO
(FEAR OF MISSING OUT)

RULE:
DON'T MISS WHAT'S GOING ON INSIDE YOU.

Ever been at home on the weekend wishing you didn't turn down that social event or opportunity having a major FOMO attack? Just in case something awesome happens.

Our Facebook friends and Instagram followings just look so damn happy at that beach/that restaurant/that party.

There is life beyond the hashtag and status feed. And FOMO isn't just with social media.

Jealousy over "Is my ex work colleague happier at their new job" or "Maybe I should be a stay at home". Comparison and FOMO is everywhere. FOMO can zap your happiness if you're not careful.

Accept the fact that someone somewhere is happier/having more fun or _____ than you. Also someone else certainly isn't.

And that's okay.

So here's some questions to ask next time you feel FOMO coming on:

Is this something I really wish I was doing?

It's okay to accept that people make different choices from your own. Be happy and secure with your choices. For example, do you really want to be at that football game in the rain when you can watch it in the comfort of home?

Do I really want to be in New York right now?

Do I really want to be being picked up in a bar tonight?

If you really, really do than ask this:

Is this FOMO feeling telling me I need to change?

Sometimes if these feelings keep happening it's a sign you need to make a different choice, that there is something deeper you are not happy with in an area of your life and there is something else you were wishing you were doing instead.

Remember though, just because something makes someone else happy doesn't mean it will for you.

And the final question:

Is this reality?

FOMO really is a lack of focus on the present because it assumes the present isn't good enough.

Instead of worrying about what's going on 'out there' or on your phone or computer, focus instead on your present moment.

You are and have chosen to be 'here' now. And you have made a good choice.

You are not missing out. There are more than enough moments to go around.

Be a role model for being resentment free as the best present you can give yourself is your own undivided attention.

FIND YOUR GEE SPOT

RULE:

YOU CAN TAP INTO YOUR PLEASURE POWER AT ANYTIME.

We all have 100 things on our list. Some remain there for years. We know if we completed some of these we would feel so empowered, happy, fulfilled.

What is it that happens to these lists that the items on them stay unresolved?

What inner demon of ours stops us ticking off our to-do's in their tracks?

Why is it that a to-do of losing weight suddenly evaporates when you see a dessert menu at a restaurant?

Or face an employer who intimidates you?

Or spend another Saturday night alone with Netflix?

Wouldn't you give your left arm almost to complete this list?

Imagine being able to create and complete your list, your goals, your resolutions, your hopes, your wishes. It's all the same.

No one tells you how to do it, nor teaches you how to fulfil your goals or tosses you in the deep end to sink or swim your way through your list. It comes from you and you alone. Feminine energy is created with our body, our thoughts and our intentions. This is our power.

So how do you cross off and accomplish this list?

It's not logic. It's pleasure. Its your Gee Spot.

When you think of something you really want, something you long for so deeply, it's not long until your logic mind shuts it down. "I can't do that. It's too hard, too much, too selfish." And even though you still want it, it gets crossed off your list mentally.

Logic is the enemy. It is limiting. It stifles us and our goals. It stunts. It says "No, you can't, its impossible."

There is nothing impossible when a woman taps into her Gee Spot to create what she wants for her life, using her mind, body and soul to get there.

It's a logical bypass.

Your Gee Spot also lies in sharing with your friends. The pleasure gets amplified. Having another woman hold your dream and support you in it adds more than just twice the energy of it becoming reality.

FILL IN THE BLANKS TO WHO YOU'RE BECOMING

RULE:
BECOME YOUR OWN HERO.

I am amazingly good at _____.

_____ comes so easily and naturally to me.

I am secretly researching, Googling and dreaming about _____

_____

when I'm supposed to be doing _____
(aka working).

If I was just my ego, I want _____

more than anything, even if it's fake and superficial.

I want to be known for _____.

If I could take a year's sabbatical and had_____

money at my disposal I would _____

and spend it on _____.

FEED YOURSELF INSPIRATION EVERYDAY

RULE:

INSPIRATION CAN BE FOUND IN EVERYDAY LIFE.

It's funny how the more we pay attention to what is around us, the more we discover and the more we want to pay attention.

Inspiration happens when we explore. When we pay attention. Exploration encourages creativity and new ideas, serendipity and invention.

Get hooked on feeding your curiosities. Get out of the routine and de-schedule your thinking. De-program and get unregimented. Make creative exploration your M.O.

Exposure yourself to pictures, words and items that inspire you. Ted X talks, books, vision boards. Things that feed your mind and soul.

It's when you're surrounded by that which inspires you, that which makes you feel that spark, it's a sign you're aligned with your purpose. Be aware of how inspiration shows up in your life. Surround yourself with what speaks to you.

BE AROUND
PEOPLE WHO MAKE
YOU DO BETTER
NOT FEEL BETTER

RULE:
SURROUND YOURSELF WITH POSITIVE PEOPLE

We become most like the people that we surround ourselves with.

If we're surround by negative energy suckers and drama queens, we and our behaviour become that. We don't feel better and we certainly don't do better.

Positive people reflect and bounce their energies onto one another. Positivity in a group of friends is an escalator.

Positivity accompanies purpose. Start doing better. Taking action. Helping others.

Start small; open the door for the person in front of you. Ask someone how their day was before telling them about yours.

Doing better gives a feeling of value that translates into positivity. And people might just appreciate you in the process.

THERE ARE NO ACCIDENTS. WE MEET PEOPLE FOR A REASON.

RULE:

WE MEET PEOPLE FOR A REASON. A SEASON. A LIFETIME.

Think about the people in your life over the years. Do they fit into one of these three categories?

Did they come at a hard time, providing support, fulfilling a need, a reason and then disappear?

Did they stay a little longer, bringing experiences, joy, happiness if only for a short time?

Or have they stayed with you, giving you a lifetime lesson?

There is an old Chinese belief of an invisible red thread that connects those around us. Destined to meet, regardless of time, place or circumstance. The thread may stretch or even tangle, but it will never break.

Sometimes you know right away that person is meant to be in your life. That they will affect your life in some profound way. Sometimes they bring with them love, joy, growth. Other times hurt, pain and unfairness.

Illness or injury. Success or downfalls. Love or lost moments. They help create who you are and who you'll become.

And most of all... Accept. Believe the realness of people in your life. Be grateful for them, however long they are meant to be a part of your journey.

DON'T MESS WITH THE GODDESS MANIFESTO

I know I am beautiful always and in all ways.

I honour other women as my tribe.

I see the good in this world and in others.

I embrace my challenges as they help me to grow.

I love and accept all parts of myself and body in thought and in action.

I experience the flow of joy in my life.

I nurture and inspire my gifts.

I believe in my wishes, dreams and the abundance of the universe.

I celebrate and am grateful for my life.

I give generously to myself, my loved ones and greater community.

I listen to my intuition and trust my inner voice.

I am open to my higher purpose.

I reclaim and own my feminine energy and divine essence.

A Final Note

Day by day, what you do is who you become. – Heraclitus

It is never too late to behave like the person you want to be, instead of continuing in a cycle of behaviour that you will regret.

What kind of person do you want to be?

Don't wait until 'next Monday' or 'January 1st' to devote yourself to that vision.

Do it now. Be it now.

This hour, today, tomorrow, at work, at play, and at home...

What you do is who you are.

ABOUT THE AUTHOR TRACEY JEWEL

Tracey Jewel is a successful woman. She won the NEIS Small Business Award in 2008, a scholarship to Rich Happy Hot Live in 2012 and was runner-up for the St George Start Up Awards in 2013. An author, professional speaker and awarded businesswoman, she's appeared on the Oprah Winfrey Show and is a regular presenter for Mind Body Spirit. She has without doubt forged her position as a role model for all women.

Tracey's interest in the female spirit began as a teenager. Fourteen years old and in love with literature, she discovered an inspirational bookstore and convinced her mother to buy her a meditation book on femininity. She was hooked, and so began her vocation in female empowerment.

Her entrepreneurial spirit was another driving force behind her rise to success. Not content with a standard high school job, Tracey accepted a position selling kitchen knives at age 16 and was the youngest in the sales team. But her age wasn't the only thing setting her apart. Applying her already impressive business intuition she ignored the door-to-door approach, instead selling directly to kitchens in cafés and restaurants, and surpassed her entire team's performance within her first week.

Her next project was an online bookstore, which she juggled with studying creative writing and marketing at Curtin University in Western Australia. Her passion for literature and femininity coupled with her natural sense of business strategy saw success come quickly, with a major bookstore purchasing the website within a short few years. Her successful business interests did not stop there, and ranged from a day spa to a book store, endeavours that brought her admiration, respect and experience.

Tracey's ability to apply sound entrepreneurial skills to transform ideas into successful business ventures has earned her a strong position in the corporate world. Passionate about marketing, she takes great excitement in seeing a campaign through to completion. From inception to success, and the follow-up analytics, she loves it all. An expert in current trends and marketing techniques, she is known for identifying the potential in a brand and transforming it into a memorable somatic marker. She believes that her job is not done until a product's success is seen in technicolour, and there is no doubt in her client's mind that her campaign has set them apart from the competition.

But her productive undercurrent remains firmly within the literary sphere. A regular writer for a number of magazines and blogs, and author of highly successful The Goddess Within, her way with words is indisputable. Her style is bold, profound and engaging, and intended to inspire others to action. Whether in a headline, an email or a book, her style is unique, enlightening and praised worldwide.

Tracey's philanthropic nature extends beyond words. She is a regular volunteer for a number of charities including Jigsaw Adoption, Esther Refuge Homes for Women, White Ribbon and the Parkerville Children's Home. Her altruism was proven in 2006 when she won a Mercedes car in a charity giveaway, but instead of accepting the prize she donated it back to the charity, earning her the nickname 'Mercedes Tracey'.

But the public Tracey Jewel isn't the full story. A lover of a little solitude, she's often found cooped up in a quirky hole-in-the-wall café, a short black in hand and her ever-present iPad and journal capturing her thoughts. And she loves being a mother, finding much joy in the time she spends with her young daughter away from the fast-paced business world.

No stranger to fame and accustomed to success, Tracey Jewel is a role model for women worldwide. Never one to take the well-worn path, she's fought her demons and persevered to build an inspiring life. But all throughout, her public-spiritedness has been strong, and each day she commits to working for the betterment of the world around her. Whether through her writing, business development or personal life, she will be remembered for her dedication to socially responsible organisations that benefit the communities around them and make a positive difference to the lives of all women.

ACKNOWLEDGEMENTS

Thanks must be given to my gorgeous girlfriends who have shared the laughs, tears and years of this books journey. Eva, Louise, Emma, Brooke, Cara, Sami, Dora, Naomi, Katie, Anita, Lucy and Mia thank you for being such beautiful Goddesses in my life and teaching me so much. Thanks to my mentor Debra Best for kicking my ass when I needed it! Thanks to my mum for always being there for me with no judgement, just a beautiful heart of gold. Thanks to all the women I have come across since my first book Goddess Within in 2011. You have taught and inspired me so much, without crossing paths this book would not exist. To the men in my life who have come into my life for a reason, a season or a lifetime, you are a part of my journey and this book. And thanks to Trudy and Scott for putting up with me and bringing my book to life, I am forever indebted to your generosity and kindness.

"50 cents of every book will be donated to the Pat Giles Centre. The Patricia Giles Centre is a feminist-based, non-profit organisation committed to providing services to women and children who have experienced or witnessed domestic violence and to men who seek to improve the quality of their family relationships."

SPECIAL THANKS TO:

Book and Tracey Jewel photography

Robbie Merritt www.robbiemerritt.com/

Beauty

Aphrodite and Apollo cosmetic clinics www.aacosmetic.com.au

Aphrodite cosmetics www.aphroditecosmetics.com.au

Hair

Naomi Panizza Creative Lengths www.creativelengths.com.au

Clothing

Shero www.sherofashion.com

Betty Tran www.bettytran.com.au

Shoes

Zamora Shoes www.zamorashoes.com.au

Jewellery

Rosendorff www.rosendorffs.com

Chimere Pearls www.chimerepearls.com.au

NOTES

NOTES

GET INSPIRED AND TAKE WEEKLY ACTION WITH TRACEY JEWEL
SUBSCRIBE AND JOIN THE 45,000 OTHERS UPPING THEIR GAME
CONTACT TRACEY – TRACEYJEWEL.COM

BOOK SIGNINGS AND WORKSHOPS

TRACEY JEWEL IS AVAILABLE FOR PRIVATE WORKSHOPS AND BOOK
EXCERPT READINGS THROUGHOUT THE WORLD.

DON'T MESS WITH GODDESS STARTER COURSE
Get your free digital course today and you'll have access to:

- The Free Course on how to make karma your bitch
- Exclusive premium articles
- A Free private webinar dishing the secrets about the "female empowerment movement"
- Many more lists, advice & goddess tools…!

PERSONAL SESSIONS

A one hour in person (Perth) or skype session to get to the
heart of any situation that is calling you. You will leave the
session feeling inspired, supported and empowered.
Sessions can include soul purpose, personal development,
strategic writing, marketing or business.

WWW.TRACEYJEWEL.COM